AF316660

Joseph Brice

THE ANSWER

Joseph Brice

"Do not forget to show hospitality to strangers, for by so doing some people have shown hospitality to angels without knowing it."

Hebrews 13:2 NIV

Credits

HOLY BIBLE:

Bible Versions:

King James Version (KJV)

New International Version (NIV)

English Standard Version (ESV)

Amplified Bible (AMP)

Contents

Preface

Dear Reader,

When you pray, remember that the supernatural burden is not on you. Your role is to attend to the natural aspect. Consider the powerful example of Jesus feeding over 5000 men, not counting the women and children who were hungry and had nothing to eat.

A young boy offered his lunch of two fish and five loaves of bread. Jesus blessed the food and instructed his disciples to distribute it to the people. Miraculously, there was an abundance of food, with baskets of leftovers. This story is a testament to the power of faith and trust in

God to provide.

Remember, in your prayers, you are not alone. You play a crucial role, but the burden is not solely on you. Your task is to bring what you have and trust that God will handle the rest. God will never demand from us what we don't possess. This understanding should bring a sense of relief. Have faith and believe that God will take care of the supernatural aspect of the prayer according to His will.

Remember, the part we can do, we should do; the things far beyond our reach are the part we give to God. It's important to understand that most of the time, our prayers will not be answered as we had in mind. This unpredictability is a testament to the divine nature of prayer and its answers.

 Be cautious not to dismiss your answered prayer simply because it doesn't align with your expectations. This is a common pitfall that many people fall into, as the religious leaders miss out on recognizing Jesus because He didn't fit their preconceived image of a messiah. Similarly, we might overlook our blessings if we are too fixated on what we think the answer should look like.

The religious leaders didn't educate Jesus. He didn't come from their social circles, religious cliques, or circle of influencers. Nor did he have material or natural wealth, which they believed was an endorsement from God. Additionally, he was not from the priestly tribe of Levy, which made the religious leaders doubt whether he was good enough to be God's much-anticipated Messiah and son despite the miracles he performed.

The religious leaders refused to accept God's answer, Jesus. They chose to wait for another messiah, ignoring all the signs that pointed towards Jesus. This story teaches us that sometimes our prejudices can blind us to the blessings and answers from God that are right in front of us.

There were times God would ask the prophet," What do you see?" This is evidence that we do not automatically see things the way God does. We should pray and ask God to open our eyes so we can see things the way He sees them. Don't let your imagination rob you of your answer.

Sometimes, we miss the answers to our prayers because we have preconceived notions about how they should appear. When the solution fails to match our expectations, we doubt its authenticity and pray to God again for an alternative answer that aligns with our imagination.

However, it's crucial to understand that the Answer to our prayers may not always come in the form we anticipate. It could be disguised in a situation we least expect or someone we never thought could offer a solution. Therefore, it's essential to keep an open mind and trust that "God's ways are higher than ours, and His thoughts are higher than ours."

When we pray, we often seek solutions to our immediate desires and needs. Yet, we must bear in mind that the effects of our prayers can extend far beyond our own lives. Our prayers might be the answer to someone else's prayers from centuries ago, underscoring the profound influence of prayer. Its responses can ignite hope and inspiration not just within us but also in those around us.

Sometimes, the quest to solve a problem can be arduous and emotionally taxing. Yet, this distress can lead us to discover a solution. Conversely, we might endeavor to solve someone else's problem without realizing that we are the solution ourselves; we might be the answer to their prayer. This interconnectedness serves as a potent reminder of the ripple effect our prayers can create.

Consider this: before Jesus went to the cross, he saw a portion of his destiny as a filled cup in a collage of tests and trials. He prayed three times that this cup would pass him, as he did not want to drink from it. God did not answer him. However, in the end, during his third request in prayer, Jesus submitted to God's will and said, "Nevertheless, not my will, but your will be done."

When life becomes challenging, and we yearn for a different answer from God, His silence can be our answer. In other words, God may not alter His will for our lives.

Have you ever wondered if the answer to a question you've been grappling with is already out there? The truth is, if we can formulate a question, God already has the answer. With God, the answer always precedes the question. He comprehends the end from the beginning and is the Alpha and Omega, the Beginning and the End, the First and the Last. It's not a coincidence that the Scripture says, "The Lamb was slain before the foundations of the world." This reaffirms God's omniscience and omnipotence, reminding us that He is perpetually in control.

This means that before humanity ever sinned, the solution to the problem was already in place. In other words, God had already provided the Answer because He is the Answer. Everything we need is in Him. He is the thirst and the water that quenches the thirst. He is the air we breathe and the lungs that desperately need it. He is the hunger and the food that satisfies. He is everything we need and more. He Is God!

Be cautious not to dismiss your answered prayer simply because it doesn't align with your expectations. This is a common pitfall that many people fall into, as The Religious Leaders known as The Pharisees miss out on recognizing Jesus because He didn't fit their preconceived image of a messiah. Similarly, we might overlook our blessings if we are too fixated on what the answer should look like.

Remember, the part we can do, we should do; the things far beyond our reach are the part we give to God.

Today, we face many challenges, and people want answers. When we pray, we should strive to have faith in God, knowing that **Jesus is The Answer!**

Chapter 1
The Miracle

The fact that you exist is nothing short of a miracle. From your conception, countless factors had to align perfectly for you to come into being. The odds of a single sperm cell successfully fertilizing an egg are incredibly low, and the timing of conception can be influenced by various factors, including the health of the parents and even external environmental factors.

Additionally, the nine-month gestation period is a marvel in and of itself, as the human body undergoes an incredible transformation to support the growth and development of a new life. Your presence today is a testament to the extraordinary resilience and strength of the human body and a reminder of just how miraculous life is.

You are a one-of-a-kind creation, designed by God and brought to life through the miracle of human reproduction. Your existence is no accident but a purposeful solution to someone's problem, a source of resolve. Embrace the beauty of your unique design and the significance of your role in the world. You are a precious gift, meant to be cherished and valued for all you are.

When we are fearful or concerned about how we are going to survive, it is common for us to become self-absorbed, focusing solely on our needs and desires. We may search for a miraculous solution to all our problems—there's nothing wrong with that. However, it's vital to remember that we are a miracle in ourselves. We may even be the answer to someone else's prayers.

Sometimes, we may overlook the blessings we have received and fail to remember how we overcame seemingly insurmountable challenges with divine intervention. "God knows our needs before we ask." It is important to remember that if God has intervened in the past, it is plausible that He can do so again, for God is eternal. "He is the same God yesterday, today, and forever more."

It is possible to be both waiting for a miracle and be a miracle for someone else simultaneously. God can use someone to help me with something that seems impossible, while I can help someone else with something that may not seem miraculous but can be the miracle they need. Therefore, we should always be aware of those around us and be ready to help them in times of need.

* * *

After all, what is life about if we do not serve others? At times, we can feel so overwhelmed by our challenges that we become paralyzed with fear, thinking we cannot overcome them. It's worth taking a step back to recognize and appreciate our uniqueness and the value we bring to this world. We are more than how much money we have, what we eat, what we wear, the house we live or the car we drive. "We are fearfully and wonderfully made."

When a baby is born, it cannot survive without its mother's support. The mother plays a crucial role as a caregiver, providing the newborn with essential nourishment, warmth, and protection. Though this responsibility may seem daunting, for most mothers, it is an act of love toward the new life they have brought into the world. Notably, this relationship between a mother and her child is a convergence of two miracles.

* * *

In this case, the mother is the miracle God used to give birth to the baby, while the baby is a miracle of life that has been born. For a mother who has longed to have a baby, the arrival of her newborn is a long-awaited answer to her prayers. Similarly, for the baby, the mother becomes the primary source of fulfillment for all its needs, including hunger, thirst, and other necessities.

For example; Moses was born into great peril. The king had ordered the death of all male Hebrew children, but his brave mother fought against this cruel decree by hiding him from the king's soldiers for three months. Despite her best efforts, she eventually had to give him up. Still, her bravery and determination made Moses one of the most influential historical figures.

The extraordinary story of Moses' birth is a

testament to the power of maternal love and unwavering faith. Despite the king's decree to put her child to death, Moses' mother did not lose hope. In an act of incredible bravery, she risked her own life to save her baby.

With nothing but her faith in God for a miracle, she crafted a small basket and set it afloat on the Nile River, entrusting her son's fate to the current. She watched her child drift away on the same river where the soldiers had thrown all of the other babies they had killed. She was sending her baby down a river where crocodiles had eaten and devoured many babies. It was like looking at a liquid graveyard for infants, the river of dead babies, a place of death and hopelessness. The river, widely known for giving and sustaining life, was now taking life.

She must have felt fear, sorrow, and hopelessness for his future. But her steadfast belief in the purpose of her child's life gave her the courage to take such a risk. This act of love and sacrifice is a testament to the strength of the human spirit and an inspiration to us all.

The basket holding baby Moses was discovered by the Pharaoh's daughter, who showed compassion for the child even though he was a Hebrew and her father had decreed that all Hebrew baby boys were to be killed. The daughter of the Pharaoh took the child into the palace, showing courage and strength to do what she believed was right, even though it was against the law of the land. In this story, two women demonstrated bravery and compassion in adversity.

Moses was born into slavery to enslaved parents. Despite this, he was raised as a prince in Egypt and received the best education. He lived a life of royalty. However, after many years, Moses committed murder and was forced to go into exile. He became alienated from all of his family and friends for many years. It may have appeared that the child of promise was a failure, now a wanted fugitive. Moses' mother and adopted mother must have been disappointed. Maybe they thought all hope was gone for Moses.

Despite these challenges, God had a plan for Moses, ultimately leading him to become a great leader and prophet. Moses' time in the land of Midian prepared him for the miracle of delivering a people who had been in bondage for over 400 years. When Moses was sent back to Egypt, he was instructed to tell Pharoah to "Let God's People Go!"

Even if your child or children are not living up to their potential, don't lose hope in them. Remember that they were a miracle when they were born, and God can perform another miracle through them. Keep praying for them and believe they are still a miracle and that God has great plans for their future.

It is crucial to educate our children about their Heavenly Father. We should be open to allowing God to use us to support, teach, and help those around us grow. Nonetheless, it's also important to remember that each one of us has been granted distinct skills and abilities, which are meant to serve a specific purpose..

For instance, Moses, who went on to write the first five books of the Bible and free an entire nation, was born to an enslaved mother who had no idea of his divine destiny. At first glance, the timing of Moses' birth appeared problematic, but it ultimately fulfilled God's plan.

Moses' life is a testimony to how God can use our problems to bring solutions and miracles. Sometimes, the answer we seek can be disguised as a problem rather than a miracle. We should not judge things based on outward appearances, for God sees and judges things of the heart.

Hannah's story is found in 1 Samuel 1: 2- 2: 22, in which an infertile woman struggles to find self-worth. She prayed so hard to God for a miracle that the preist assumed she was drunk. Despite her being misunderstood and wrongfully judged even in the house of God, she became a testament to the power of faith and prayer. She suffered years of being unable to conceive, she never lost hope and continued to trust in God. Finally, God blessed her with a son he was named Samuel, meaning, "God has heard."Hannah didn't take this miracle for granted.

Hannah nurtured and protected Samuel, raising him to be a faithful servant of God. She was so grateful for this miracle that she made a vow to give Samuel back to God when he was old enough to serve Him. Her son would become one of the most significant prophets in the Bible, anointing Israel's first king, Saul, and Israel's greatest king, David. Hannah's unwavering faith and devotion to God inspire us all.

When a child is born, we have no clue what they may be or become. God, who is the All-Knowing God, is the only One who knows. The most outstanding achievement for the child is to become what God created them to be. Although we may benefit from having the child, we must remember they belong to God, and He will make us accountable while seeing them through.

Don't let problems or burdens discourage you, for they may be the very things that lead to your miracle. With unwavering faith in God and a commitment to finding the answer, you can turn your challenges into blessings. Remember, the solution may not be apparent at first, but keep an open mind and trust the process. Your miracle is waiting for you to claim it.

Chapter 2
When We Pray

Have you ever prayed for something and later realized that the answer you got was not what you expected? It can be confusing, even frustrating. Maybe you rejected the answer and prayed again, thinking this couldn't be from God. We must learn to bow to God's will.

We often seek solutions to our immediate wants and needs when we pray. However, we should not forget that the effects of our prayers can go beyond our own lives. Our prayers may be the answer to someone else's prayers from centuries ago, so we should not underestimate the power of prayer. Its answers can bring hope and inspiration to ourselves and those around us.

You may possess certain qualities or skills that could help someone else solve a problem or find an answer to a question. You might be the missing piece that someone needs to complete a puzzle, the solution to a challenge they are facing, or the source of guidance they require. You never know how your actions or words might impact someone else's life, so always strive to be helpful, kind, and supportive. You could be the answer that someone has been searching for.

The Apostle Paul once disclosed that he prayed to God three times, asking Him to remove the 'thorn in his side.' Paul believed that the removal of the thorn would be the answer to his prayers. However, while waiting, the Lord responded, "My grace is sufficient for you."

It's common to feel disheartened when we see God answering prayers we've prayed for someone else while our requests seem to be left unanswered. This can be perplexing, mainly when eagerly awaiting a specific outcome. It's important to remember that God's plans are not always what we expect, and our prayers are being heard and answered in ways that are best for us, even if we can't see them yet.

Paul never expected to gain a deep understanding of grace by embodying God's model of love, mercy, and grace. This experience turned out to be an answer to his prayers. Often, we plead with God to remove uncomfortable situations from our lives, but He may use those situations to help us grow and become a source of hope and inspiration for others. You might be the answer to someone's prayers. At times, we may encounter challenges that feel like "thorns."

Difficulties, struggles, and hardships are

part of life. It's important to remember that if God chooses not to remove these obstacles, it may be because He wants to use them to make us a testimony. Our experiences and how we handle them can inspire and encourage others who may be going through similar struggles. Therefore, we should trust God's plan and use our thorns to testify to His love and faithfulness.

Sometimes, we miss the answers to our prayers because we have preconceived notions about how they should appear. When the solution fails to match our expectations, we doubt its authenticity and pray to God again for an alternative answer that aligns with our imagination. However, it's crucial to understand that the answer to our prayers may not always come in the form we anticipate. It could be disguised in a situation we least expect or someone we never thought could offer a solution. Therefore, it's essential to keep an open mind and trust that "God's ways are higher than ours, and His thoughts are higher than ours."

When John the Baptist came preaching about repentance and baptism, the Pharisees, who knew the prophecy of making the crooked paths straight, rejected him. Even though they witnessed something extraordinary, they could not reconcile John's teachings with their preconceived ideas, causing them to reject his message.

It is important to note that even astute men with knowledge of God's Word can miss important details. This emphasizes the significance of always praying and demonstrating humility before God, even when the answer may seem obvious. Seeking God's guidance may be challenging, but it is necessary as it ultimately benefits us and brings glory to God.

Prayer is a highly individual practice that is

unique to each person, like our DNA or fingerprints. It is a way of communicating with God, allowing us to express our deepest thoughts, desires, and fears. However, prayer is not just about making requests or seeking divine intervention. It is also about developing and maintaining a close relationship with God.

Prayer is a practice that requires trust, honesty, and consistent communication. Prayer is about being open and vulnerable with God, much like how we would be with a caring parent. Through prayer, we use a language that goes beyond words and is understood by the heart. In the same way that a mother understands the needs of her newborn without words, God understands our needs and desires through our presence and the emotions we express while we pray.

The act of prayer is not about making lengthy declarations and proclamations. Instead, it's about recognizing humanity's humility. It involves entrusting oneself to the care of an infinite God who bears our infirmities and cares for us. As we grow and mature, we should not just request God's assistance; as dutiful children, we should be willing to contribute to God's vision and purpose.

Looking forward to reuniting with Him in the next world is also essential to prayer.

It's a common trend that people only reach out to others when they require something, without bothering to communicate when things are going well. This behavior is alarming, and it raises the question of how many individuals fall into this category. It's surprising how little thought is given to the fact that others may also need something or appreciate an expression of love.

Nobody wants to be thought of solely when something is required from them. Many of us are guilty of treating God like a mere tool or Genie, someone who should grant our wishes. It's not uncommon for people to feel upset with God when His response is not what we expect as if we're deserving or worthy of it. Such behavior is unacceptable, and we should strive to conduct ourselves with more excellent poise and reverence.

It can be frustrating when someone sends a message or text without any greetings or pleasantries and directly asks for money by saying, "I need some money." This behavior can be seen as a lack of respect and basic manners. Many of us treat God in the same manner. It is important to remember that this behavior can also be perceived as disrespectful to God, who is our Creator and knows our needs before we ask. When Jesus was asked to teach us how to pray, He emphasized the importance of showing gratitude and respect to God.

"And when you pray, you must not be like the hypocrites, for they love to stand and pray in the synagogues and at the street corners so that they may be seen by others. Truly, I can say to you that they have received their reward. But when you pray, go into your room and shut the door and pray to your Father, who is in secret. And your Father, who sees you in secret, will reward you.

"And when you pray, do not heap up empty phrases as the Gentiles do, for they think that they will be heard for their many words. Do not be like them, for your Father knows what you need before you ask him.

Pray then like this: "Our Father in heaven, hallowed be your name. Your kingdom come, your will be done, on earth as it is in heaven. Give us this day our daily bread, and forgive us our debts, as we also have forgiven our debtors. And lead us not into temptation, but deliver us from evil. Matthew 6:5-13:

* * *

On another occasion, Jesus prayed and said, " Father, give me the glory I once had when I was with you before the foundations of the world. Glorify your Son that your Son may glorify You.

Jesus prayed this prayer when it was time for the next level of the supernatural when it was time to deal with death, which was the greatest enemy. Before praying for Lazarus to come out of the tomb, he prayed this prayer because Jesus would later resurrect himself. Jesus knew that for this, the anointing was not enough. Maybe for your next level, you may need God's holy.

When you pray, remember you are not responsible for the miracle or the supernatural. Your responsibility is the natural part. For instance, when Jesus preached to a multitude of 5000 people who were hungry and had nothing to eat, a young boy with two fish and five loaves of bread was present. Jesus prayed over the food, blessed it, and then instructed his disciples to distribute it to the people.

There was more than enough food, with

baskets left over. Therefore, no matter what situation you are going through, remember that you are not responsible for God's part in the prayer. Bring what you have to God, and have faith that He will do the part you cannot.

Before Jesus went to the cross, he saw his tests and trials as a filled cup. He prayed three times that this cup would pass him, as he did not want to drink from it. God did not answer him. However, in the end, during his third request in prayer, he submitted to God's will and said, "Nevertheless, not my will, but your will be done." Sometimes, when things get hard, and we feel we want another answer from God, His silence can be our answer. In other words, God may not change His mind concerning His will for our lives.

"Dear Lord, I am facing difficult times and challenges that have left me feeling defeated. I know that I am anointed, but in this situation, I feel the anointing alone is not enough to help me overcome my enemies and rise above my circumstances. I humbly ask you to grant me your glory so that I can break free from this grave that I find myself in.

* * *

You may be struggling with your finances, marriage, divorce, children, relationships overall, or maybe a job or no job at all. It could be your peace or joy. Whatever it is, you need divine intervention to resurrect from this challenging situation.

 Please grant me your glory, Lord so that I may glorify your name, Jesus.

Chapter 3

In the Waiting

When we pray and ask God for something, we often have no idea how He will answer or in what form our answer will come. One of the most significant challenges to our faith is waiting for His reply. It is during this waiting period that we must determine whether or not we will remain faithful. Sometimes, when we receive a prophetic word or promise from God, we become anxious and impatient, wanting to hurry the process as if God needed our help.

The more significant the promise or blessing, the greater the tests and the waiting period. Many people tend to get disheartened during this waiting period and give up on their dreams. When you have been waiting for a long time for something God has promised you, you may lose many things, including friends, family, resources, and relationships. Some may even think you are crazy for not giving up or quitting.

When Abram was ninety-nine, the Lord appeared to him and said, "I am God Almighty; walk before me and be blameless. I will confirm my covenant between me and you and will greatly increase your numbers." Abram fell facedown, and God said to him, "As for me, this is my covenant with you: You will be the father of many nations. No longer will you be called Abram; your name will be Abraham, for I have made you a father of many nations. I will make you very fruitful; I will make nations of you, and kings will come from you. I will establish my covenant as an everlasting covenant between me and you and your descendants after you for the generations to come, to be your God and the God of your descendants after you.

The whole land of Canaan, where you are now an alien, I will give as an everlasting possession to you and your descendants after you, and I will be their God." Then God said to Abraham, "As for you, you must keep my covenant, you and your descendants after you for the generations to come. This is my covenant with you and your descendants after you, the covenant you are to keep: Every male among you shall be circumcised. You are to undergo circumcision, and it will be the sign of the covenant between me and you. For the generations to come, every male among you who is eight days old must be circumcised, including those born in your household or bought with money from a foreigner–those who are not your offspring. Whether born in your household or bought with your money, they must be circumcised. My covenant in your flesh is to be an everlasting covenant. Genesis

17:1-13 NIV

The story of Abram and Sarai, who later became Abraham and Sarah, is a remarkable account of faith, patience, and obedience to God. God promised them a child, but as the years went by, they grew old and still had no child. However, their wait was not in vain, as God was using this time to transform them into the people they needed to be to receive the promise He had made to them.

They learned to trust God even when things seemed impossible, and their faith was strengthened through the waiting process. Abraham and Sarah thought they were ready for the promise, but God had a more excellent plan. He wanted to produce something that would last for generations to come. He was interested in giving them a child and creating a nation and a people that would bear His name and fulfill His purposes.

After a long wait, Abraham and Sarah were finally blessed with a son named Isaac. His birth was nothing short of a miracle. Isaac became the father Jacob of the 12 tribes of Israel, who are known today as the Jewish people. God's promise to Abraham and Sarah was not just for them but for their future generations. Even today, thousands of years later, God's plan for Abraham's descendants continues to bear fruit. When we face difficult situations, many of us find comfort and guidance in trusting and believing in God.

When we encounter challenging situations, we often seek someone to rely on and trust. However, it can be difficult to trust an entity we cannot see or touch, especially regarding God. Nonetheless, it is crucial to keep in mind that choosing to trust and believe in God can lead us to experience something truly remarkable. By not trusting and believing in God, we may never know the extent of the incredible outcome that could have been possible. This is why we need the Holy Spirit to help us.

By having faith that God will make good on his promises to us, we allow ourselves to be open to receiving the answers we seek. This can lead to peace and comfort, knowing we are not alone in facing life's challenges. So, if we choose not to trust and believe in God, we may never know just how great *The Answer* to our prayers could be.

The story of Joseph from the Bible tells us about a young man who was betrayed by his brothers and sold into slavery. After that, he was falsely accused and sent to prison. However, Joseph's ability to interpret dreams eventually led him to be called upon by the Pharaoh to interpret his dreams. Joseph became known as the Dreamer and helped others understand the meaning of their dreams.

Sometimes, we may not understand people who are different from us, but we should remember that they may have been called to be that way for a purpose, which is to be ready when God's will is fulfilled in their lives.

Some people may appear strange or different from others on a journey of self-discovery, which is necessary to understand their life's purpose and what is expected of them. Serving others is considered a divine calling and can be challenging, as seen in the example of Jesus, who was referred to as the suffering servant. Those called to serve others may face hardships and difficulties, even from the people they are trying to help.

The account of Joseph's brothers' betrayal and the sale of him into slavery has been documented in the Book of Genesis. The narrative recounts how the brothers, disconcerted by Joseph's dreams that indicated his eventual exaltation, plotted to kill him.

However, they eventually decided to sell him to a caravan of Ishmaelite/Midianite traders who were passing through.

The Ishmaelites were well-known for their trade, and the brothers offered to sell Joseph to them for 20 pieces of silver. The Ishmaelites purchased Joseph and took him to Egypt to sell him for a profit. The Ishmaelites were unaware that Joseph was, in fact, their blood relative, descended from Abraham, their forefather, four generations later. The Ishmaelites were merely conducting business and were unaware of Joseph's familial connection with his captors.

Hagar, the mother of Ishmael, was exiled to the wilderness with her son. An angel appeared to Hagar and conveyed that God would bless her son and his descendants, who would grow into a great nation. Ultimately, they settled in the Midian region and became known as the Midianites, distinguished by their place of residence, while their patrilineal lineage identified them as Ishmaelites.

Joseph played a key role in rescuing his family during a famine that claimed many lives. His father, Jacob, was later renamed Israel, and his 12 sons were responsible for creating a nation of people called the Israelites, who are known as Jews today. It's incredible to think they were the answer to generations of people. We continue to read, study, teach, and preach about their stories.

This is the lineage of Abraham, Isaac, Jacob, and Joseph from the Old Testament. God promised Abraham that he would be blessed and become the father of many nations. Abraham's son Ishmael, whose mother was Haggai, and Isaac, whose mother was Sarah, carried forward his legacy.

Jacob, one of Isaac's sons, had 12 sons. One of them was Joseph, who became the second most powerful man in the world at that time.

Joseph's divine revelation and wisdom saved countless lives during a harsh famine, including the kingdom of Egypt. This famine brought the Ishmaelites and Isaac's bloodline together. The Ishmaelites rescued Joseph and eventually saved his brother's bloodline.

The story of Joseph in the Bible teaches us the importance of having a positive attitude and helping others. Joseph's brothers hated him for reasons they didn't understand, but it was because he was the answer to their unrevealed problems. Later, when they faced a severe famine, Joseph answered their problems.

The story of Joseph teaches us a valuable lesson. If he had let the injustices he faced make him bitter and resentful, he would have missed out on his blessings. This reminds us that even when things don't go as expected or wanted, it's essential to stay positive and trust that everything happens for a reason. We can also bring blessings and success into our lives by helping others and being open to their dreams.

We tend to focus only on our problems during the most difficult times. If you are currently facing a challenging situation, it's important to remember that there may be a bigger picture that you're not aware of yet. Perhaps the challenges you're facing are part of your personal growth and development and will help you become the solution to someone else's problem. While some may view you as a problem, it's important to remember that God sees you as the answer.

How often have you heard someone say, 'I know I'm here for a reason (purpose)'? You need to listen to God long enough to know that purpose. The purpose will keep knocking at your door even if you don't want to answer it. When God calls you, don't expect everyone to hear what you hear. We must trust Him enough to keep walking even in "the valley of the shadow of death, fearing no evil because God is with us."

The Bible also mentions the story of Moses, who was saved from Pharaoh by a Midianite priest, the descendant of Ishmael. Moses later married the daughter of this priest and became a shepherd for 40 years before God called him to lead the Israelites out of Egypt. It is remarkable how God's plan unfolds in mysterious ways, orchestrating events that span generations and bloodlines. Despite the appearance of abandonment, God is always there, guiding His people to fulfill His will.

The early life of Moses was one of luxury and privilege, having been raised in a palace. However, at the age of forty, he made a decision that would lead to his exile for the next four decades. This decision was prompted by the fact that Moses had committed a crime, namely, the murder of a man. As a result, he found himself on Pharaoh's list of most wanted individuals and was forced to flee to a distant land, Midian, where he would reside for the next forty years.

Notably, no record exists of any conversation or divine encounter between Moses and God during this period. It is thus conceivable that Moses may have felt that he had compromised whatever destiny his life was meant to fulfill. He was, in effect, a fugitive from justice. Moses, despite his education and royal background, found himself in the humbling position of a shepherd in the fields of Midian. The Egyptian culture viewed shepherds with disdain, as they were considered uneducated and beneath their social status.

Shepherding, as a profession, entailed physical labor, patience, and a great deal of dirt. Moses, who had once held high status, now spent his days watching someone else's sheep to provide for his family. The enemy indeed plagued Moses' mind, reminding him of who he used to be and how low he had fallen. Unbeknownst to him, God had a more excellent plan for Moses' life, requiring him to be humbled so that God could receive the glory. Moses' journey from a high-ranking prince to a lowly shepherd teaches us that sometimes, we must be stripped of our pride and ego to fulfill our true purpose.

After spending four decades in the palace, Moses spent another forty years in the wilderness, devoting himself to shepherding. It was during this time that he was called upon by God, who manifested himself in the form of a burning bush that remained unconsumed by the flames. When Moses proceeded to investigate the site, he encountered the God he had been taught about and had heard about but had not yet known for himself. Until then, his knowledge of God had been second-hand, passed down from others.

Chapter 4
The Assignment

When Moses saw the burning bush, he was not the only one who saw it. However, he was the only one who responded to it. This quote, 'Many are called, but few are chosen,' means that those who respond to the call and dedicate themselves to the voice that called them are chosen.

Moses didn't even know what name to address God as. What is your name? How should I answer the people when I go to Egypt to tell them you called me and have sent me to deliver them from the bondage of slavery?

What will I say, Moses asked God. "I AM THAT I AM," God said to Moses. Tell them I AM," said God.

When presented with the task of returning to Egypt, Moses was overcome with fear, knowing that he was a wanted man due to an unresolved murder charge. However, God reassured Moses that he need not worry about the outstanding warrant, as all those seeking him were no longer alive. "Fear not, Moses, for I am with you," proclaimed the Lord God.

Moses, an essential figure in the world's religious history, embarked on a mission to deliver God's people from Egypt. His journey was filled with challenges, as he was met with resistance from those who did not accept his authority. God intervened and inflicted ten plagues on Pharaoh and Egypt, which eventually led to the release of the Israelites.

The journey to the promised land was

difficult, as they wandered in the wilderness for 40 years. During this time, Moses authored the first five books of the Bible, also known as the Torah. The books, which include Genesis, Exodus, Leviticus, Numbers, and Deuteronomy, were written over several years while Moses led the Israelites through the wilderness. Remarkably, these books have stood the test of time and remain relevant today.

Moses is credited with overseeing the construction of the Tabernacle, formulating the Ten Commandments, and establishing the Passover Feast, which is widely regarded as one of the most significant religious observances of the year. As part of this ritual, God instructed Moses to apply lamb's blood to the doorposts and lintels of homes, which would serve as a sign to the death angel to "pass over" the households so marked.

This tradition continues today as a symbol

of faith and divine protection with the Passover feasts. This is done in remembrance of how God delivered them as a people out of the bondage of slavery and abuse.

The story of Moses is an inspiring example of how we can be a source of help and support for others, even when we struggle to find answers. Despite his flaws and past mistakes, God did not waver in his belief in Moses or his purpose. When Moses had given up hope and accepted his life as it was, destiny called him to become a deliverer and prophet for a nation in need. This story teaches us the important lesson that our past should not define our future and that we should never give up on our purpose in life.

Despite enduring immense suffering and significant sacrifices, Moses' contributions to the world's religious history are undeniable. Despite his challenges and years off the grid, Moses remains essential in developing and propagating various religious beliefs. The Mosaic Laws have played an instrumental role in shaping the cultures of numerous societies. It is remarkable to consider how Moses' mother could have foreseen that her son would be the chosen one by God to deliver their people from over 400 years of bondage.

The divine call to answer someone's dilemma or problem has been universally recognized as a significant responsibility. It is imperative to comprehend that each of us possesses the potential to be a solution for someone. Often, we become excessively engrossed in our predicaments, which may cause us to overlook that we are the solution to someone else's problem. How many times have we said, "Jesus is the answer?" We can sing that and say that now, but during Jesus' time, many thought of him as the problem, a false prophet, and rejected him.

"Jesus returned to Galilee in the power of

the Spirit, and news about him spread through the whole countryside. He taught in their synagogues, and everyone praised him. He went to Nazareth, where he had been brought up, and on the Sabbath day, he went into the synagogue, as was his custom. And he stood up to read.

The scroll of the prophet Isaiah was handed to him. Unrolling it, he found the place where it is written: "The Spirit of the Lord is on me because he has anointed me to preach good news to the poor. He has sent me to proclaim freedom for the prisoners and recovery of sight for the blind, to release the oppressed, to proclaim the year of the Lord's favor."

Then he rolled up the scroll, gave it back to the attendant, and sat down. The eyes of everyone in the synagogue were fastened on him, and he began by saying to them, "Today, this scripture is fulfilled in your hearing." All spoke well of him and were amazed at the gracious words that came from his lips. "Isn't this Joseph's son?" they asked. Jesus said to them, "Surely you will quote this proverb to me: 'Physician, heal yourself! Do here in your hometown what we have heard that you did in Capernaum.' " "I tell you the truth," he continued, "no prophet is accepted in his hometown."   Luke 4:14-24

Unfortunately, some individuals cannot see beyond their preconceived notions and biases, preventing them from recognizing the potential in others. The Israelites had been following the teachings of Moses and the prophets for a long time, which had given them an understanding of the signs that would indicate the arrival of the Messiah.

Chapter 5
The Rejection

Despite Jesus fulfilling these criteria, they were more interested in a king like David or Solomon, who would bring wealth and glory to their earthly kingdom. However, Nazareth, where Jesus was from, was a humble and impoverished place.

"I assure you that there were many widows in Israel in Elijah's time when the sky was shut for three and a half years, and there was a severe famine throughout the land. Yet Elijah was not sent to any of them but to a widow in Zarephath in the region of Sidon. And there were many in Israel with leprosy in the time of

Elisha the prophet, yet not one of them was cleansed–only Naaman the Syrian."

All the people in the synagogue were furious when they heard this. They got up, drove him out of the town, and took him to the brow of the hill on which the city was built in order to throw him down the cliff. But he walked right through the crowd and went on his way. Then he went down to Capernaum, a town in Galilee, and on the Sabbath began to teach the people. They were amazed at his teaching because his message had authority".   Luke 4:25-32

The historical text speaks of Jesus being rejected by his people and how he went to Capernaum. The people were amazed at his message and admired how he preached with authority. This raises an essential point about ministry - sometimes, we may feel like we need more of God's anointing to deal with certain people, but the truth is that we need to change the people we are ministering to. It is not always a matter of increasing one's anointing but instead finding someone hungry for God's word and respecting our anointing. The anointing that we appreciate is the anointing that we will benefit from.

Interestingly, it is said that Jesus could not do many mighty works in his hometown of Nazareth because of their unbelief. However, in Capernaum, he performed many mighty works because the people there believed in him. This highlights the importance of faith when it comes to receiving from God. It is essential to highlight that during the time of Jesus, the people of Nazareth had a negative perception of him and his mother, Mary. Some even went as far as to tarnish their reputation and question their legitimacy.

It is worth noting that Jesus' paternity, like King David's, was also a topic of discussion and debate among the people at that time.

Jesus' teachings and actions have been the subject of numerous controversies throughout history. Nevertheless, the impact of his teachings has been remarkable, and his sacrifice is considered an eternal contribution to humanity. His teachings have played a significant role in shaping the moral and ethical values of many cultures worldwide. His love, forgiveness, and compassion message has inspired countless individuals and continues influencing today's world.

The crucifixion and death of Jesus Christ are regarded as the ultimate sacrifice for the redemption of humankind's sins. The act of atonement was a painful offering that was presented to God and accepted. Jesus, who was without sin, became a sin for humanity. All the sins of the world were nailed to the cross, and through his death and resurrection, Jesus provided a way for believers to be forgiven and reconciled with God.

When serpents bit the Children of Israel, the Lord God instructed Moses to make a brazen serpent and put it on a pole. The people were to gather and look up at it. He told Moses to lift it before them and said He would heal them of their snakebites."

Jesus said, "Just as Moses lifted up the snake in the wilderness, so the Son of Man must be lifted up, that everyone who believes may have eternal life in him." 3:14

The good news is that we can find true vindication and justice through Christ's redemption and restoration. It's incredible to think that despite the wrongs we may have suffered, there is hope for restoration and healing.

Through the power of the cross and the shedding of his blood, Jesus has freed us from the burden of sin. His love and sacrifice are the inspiration that draws us towards him, and it is through these actions that our souls are redeemed.

You become a witness when you experience Jesus' love, forgiveness, and power for yourself. The Holy Spirit compels you to speak about His goodness and what He has done for you, thereby lifting Him. You become the right voice, vindicated from the judgment of obeying the wrong voice. So, raise your voice and let the world know what you used to be and what you have done. You have been changed.

Change the way you see yourself; I know it's challenging. Stop focusing on your problems and start seeing you the way God sees you. You're not the problem without a solution, but the solution for the problem lies within you. You are the answer to your generation. You can only see your true self by seeing how great the One who created you is.

God, The Creator, created you to be The

Answer.

This speaks about Satan's desire to have a hold on the old version of ourselves, the one who was rebellious and disobedient to God. It emphasizes the importance of knowing who we are listening to and following, regardless of whether we consider ourselves saved.

Chapter 6
Faith to Obey

"It takes faith to obey God!"

The enemy knows that if we surrender to God, we will obey whatever He commands. The prophecy in the garden foretold the crushing of Satan's head at the cost of someone's heel being bruised for having the courage to stomp on the devil's head. We get to see how Jesus exposes the devil's intentions and tactics.

And the Lord said, Simon, Simon, behold, Satan hath desired to have you, that he may sift you as wheat: But I have prayed for thee, that thy faith fail not: and when thou art converted, strengthen thy brethren. Luke 22:31

Have you ever noticed how Jesus addressed Simon as his original name, not Peter? This was to let Simon know that Jesus knew exactly who he was talking to at the time. Peter wanted to do what was right, but Simon, his birth name and nature, was associated with the flesh. This name was produced because of the curse that came upon the ground for man's sake, and since the body is made from the ground, it is associated with the curse. However, God did not curse the spirit of man. Some people talk about getting rid of generational curses, but Jesus came to deal with the curse from its root, which covers all curses. When Jesus died on the cross, he could remove the curse from its source.

This means that through faith in Jesus, individuals can be free from their family history's adverse effects and be restored to a new life. It's important to remember that troubles and persecutions are a part of life, and it doesn't mean your family is cursed more than others. Most families may know how to keep their secrets hidden, making it seem like they don't have any curses.

Jesus once said, "'I have prayed that your faith won't fail you." He knew that the work would be completed at the cross. Remember, the devil may try to use everything in his power to get to you, but always keep in mind that he is after your faith. Stay strong and hold on to it." The enemy knows that your faith is your access granted to the new and powerful you.

Don't allow people to persuade or flatter your flesh while Satan is seeking to destroy your soul. What is your purpose in being here? We need to understand our purpose and focus on fulfilling it. When we identify what we were created to do, we can align our actions with our true calling and, in turn, bring glory to God.

Discovering our purpose can bring clarity and direction to our lives and help us lead a more fulfilling and meaningful existence. So, it's essential to reflect on our passions, talents, and strengths and find ways to use them to serve others and positively impact the world.

If we manage to reach the converted part, Satan loses power over us. His mission is to keep spiritual leaders, pastors, and preachers as worldly and carnal as the ungodly. The devil doesn't care about your race, religion, gender, or any other personal characteristic; he is only interested in hindering you from fulfilling your divine purpose. The bigger your calling and mission, the greater your opposition.

Many people have abandoned God due to pressure from loved ones and friends, like Simon or Judas. In such moments of questioning, it's important to remember that

God is faithful and to reflect on what God has entrusted you with.

Satan may try to corrupt our hearts and minds, hindering us from fulfilling our mission. Jesus knew that Simon (the old nature) would deny him, but Peter (the new man) could never. Simon is from the dust of the earth, while Peter, the apostle, is the called servant from the kingdom of heaven; his spirit man knows God.

He's been covered by the blood. The enemy knew Peter was chosen to be in charge of the newly born church, so he desperately sought to destroy Simon so that Peter would never come forth.

We often believe we need many things to please God, but this is untrue. We can please God by obeying Him and coming to Him honestly and transparently, which means that whatever we have and are, we acknowledge that it is all from God.

Chapter 7
The Answer

David received a prophecy that he would become the King of Israel. Everything seemed to work out in his favor for a while, but then things turned for the worse. King Saul became his enemy and tried to kill him. To save his life, David had to flee, and he spent over ten years in exile. During this time, he settled in enemy territory in Ziklag with 600 men.

One day, upon returning from battle, they found that their city had been burned down, and all their possessions, wives, and children were gone. Frustrated and angry, the men turned on David, blaming him for the tragedy, and even considered stoning him. Despite the difficult circumstances, David remained committed to the prophecy, which was taking an unexpected turn.

According to the Bible, David wept until no more tears were left. He then prayed and asked the Lord for guidance on what to do next. The Lord replied, instructing David to pursue his enemy and promising that he would recover all that he had lost. David and his army set out to find their enemy without a clear destination.

However, 200 of David's 600 men felt too weak to fight and refused to continue. As David and his remaining men pursued their enemy, they came across a young man who appeared to be dead. David went to tend to him and discovered that he was still alive. He offered him food and drink to help him recover.

David asked him," Who do you belong to,

and where do you come from?"

He said, " I am an Egyptian, slave of an Amelekite. My master abandoned me when I became ill three days ago. We raided several cities, and we burned Ziklag." David asked, "Can you lead me down to this party?"

He answered, "Swear to me before God that you will not kill me. Or hand me over to my master, and I will take you to them." He led David to the camp, where they saw their wives and children unharmed. David and his men fought the Amalekites from dusk until the next day's evening. They successfully recovered everything that the Amalekites had taken, including the women and children. Nothing was missing, whether young or old. David claimed it all and said, "This is David's spoils." After this victory, David never struggled financially again.

David was unaware that the individual he

was assisting was part of the group that had raided his city and taken away their wives and children. However, this person gave him directions and valuable information on where to find his people and possessions. This information brought great relief to David and his fellow men, who had been tormented by thoughts of their loved ones being dead.

What if we were too preoccupied with our issues to care for someone in need? It's easy to overlook a stranger who may not share our race or social status. But what if we could all be like David, who had a compassionate heart? Sometimes, the answer to our prayers comes disguised as a problem, and we may never know our answer if we are not willing to be someone else's answer. Let's strive to be someone's answer, just like David was for the young man he helped.

To be at peace with whatever God calls us to do, we must understand His will for our lives and avoid envying our neighbors. When we get this right, we become the answer to someone's prayer, even if they don't see it or appreciate you. Jesus came to this world as our answer, but will we believe him?

"Who hath believed our report?

and to whom is the arm of the LORD revealed?

For he shall grow up before him as a tender plant,

and as a root out of a dry ground:

he hath no form nor comeliness;

and when we shall see him, there is no beauty that we should

desire him.

He is despised and rejected of men;

a man of sorrows and acquainted with grief:

and we hid as it were our faces from him;

he was despised, and we esteemed him not.

Surely he hath borne our griefs,

and carried our sorrows:

yet we did esteem him stricken,

smitten of God and afflicted.

But he was wounded for our transgressions,

he was bruised for our iniquities:

the chastisement of our peace was upon
him;

and with his stripes, we are healed.

All we, like sheep, have gone astray;

we have turned every one to his own way;

and the LORD hath laid on him the iniquity of us all.

He was oppressed, and he was afflicted,

yet he opened not his mouth:

he is brought as a lamb to the slaughter,

and as a sheep before her shearers is dumb,

so he openeth not his mouth.

He was taken from prison and from judgment:

and who shall declare his generation?

for he was cut off out of the land of the living:

for the transgression of my people was he stricken.

And he made his grave with the wicked,

and with the rich in his death;

because he had done no violence,

neither was any deceit in his mouth.

Yet it pleased the LORD to bruise him; he hath put

him to grief: when thou shalt make his soul an offering

for sin, he shall see his seed, he shall prolong his days,

and the pleasure of the LORD shall prosper in his hand". Isaiah   53:1-10

Around 700 years before the birth of Jesus Christ, the prophet Isaiah predicted the arrival of the Messiah. Despite possessing the necessary qualities and fulfilling the prophecies, Jesus faced a lot of disbelief and rejection from the people. The reason for their skepticism and disapproval can be attributed to their preconceived ideas about the Messiah's physical appearance and intellectual abilities, which Jesus did not conform to.

Although Jesus faced many challenges during his time on Earth, he persevered and continued his mission. He is a testament to the power of determination and willpower in adversity. Jesus encountered opposition from various groups, most notably the Pharisees, who were religious leaders. They made his path difficult and demonstrated hatred towards him, ultimately contributing to his death. Despite this opposition, Jesus remained steadfast in his teachings, spreading love and forgiveness.

"We believe that Jesus is the ultimate solution to our problems, but seeing how people treated him is disheartening. Despite being the answer to all of their questions, he was mistreated, abused, misunderstood, and rejected. He was despised, cast down, hated, lied on, falsely accused, betrayed, arrested, condemned, and judged. God sent his only son to save the world, but unfortunately, many people didn't receive him or believe that he was the Messiah. Many today continue not to believe, although the signs are all around us. Many are waiting for another answer.

Despite knowing the scriptures and prophecies about Jesus, they refused to accept him because he did not fit their preconceived idea of The Answer to their long-awaited prayers. While he was dying on the cross, Jesus made a plea to his father to forgive those who were responsible for his crucifixion, as they did not realize the gravity of their actions. He did so, hoping some would repent and be saved.

This act of extending grace beyond death and the grave was a testament to his compassion and love for humanity. Thankfully, some of them did repent and were publicly acknowledged as followers of Jesus by getting baptized and receiving the Holy Ghost.

"'The Lord said to my Lord, "Sit at my right hand until I make your enemies your footstool."Let all the house of Israel therefore know for certain that God has made him both Lord and Christ, this Jesus whom you crucified."

Now, when they heard this, they were cut to the heart and said to Peter and the rest of the apostles, "Brothers, what shall we do?" And Peter said to them, "Repent and be baptized every one of you in the name of Jesus Christ for the forgiveness of your sins, and you will receive the gift of the Holy Spirit. For the promise is for you and your children and for all who are far off, everyone whom the Lord our God calls to himself.

And with many other words, he bore witness and continued to exhort them, saying, "Save yourselves from this crooked generation." So those who received his word were baptized, and there were added that day about three thousand souls. "   Acts 2:34-41

The message of the kingdom being preached and the price that Jesus paid for our salvation can transform our hearts. Jesus knew that, in time, countless souls would be touched by the power of God's love and mercy. Even if it takes a while for someone to grasp the message, what's important is that they ultimately do. This is why Jesus came to this world - to bring hope and redemption to all who seek it.

Their hearts changed as soon as they heard the message of the kingdom being preached and learned about the price Jesus had paid for their salvation. Jesus was aware that, over time, many hearts would be touched by God's love and mercy. It doesn't matter when someone comes to understand it as long as they do eventually. This is precisely why Jesus came to this world.

It is crucial to remember that forgiveness can be a powerful tool to liberate oneself from hurt and pain caused by others. Even if someone has caused deep hurt to you, forgiving them can free you from carrying that pain with you for the rest of your life. By forgiving those who have wronged you, you can create space in your heart and mind for healing and growth. This can help you avoid negative emotions from controlling your thoughts and actions.

It is crucial to understand that forgiveness does not imply forgetting or excusing the harm done to you. Instead, forgiveness means accepting the damage caused while releasing the anger, resentment, and bitterness that can arise from holding onto grudges. By forgiving others, you can liberate yourself from the negative emotions that prevent you from experiencing true peace and happiness.

If you end up in heaven, you may encounter people who have wronged you in the past but ended up giving their lives to the Lord Jesus in time. By forgiving them now, you can prevent any unexpected feelings of shock or surprise at their presence and move ahead with a clean heart and mind. Choosing to forgive can help you release yourself from the burden of grudges and move towards a brighter future. This can also help you feel more at peace with the belief that God will forgive you, even in difficult times of injustice and hardships.

It is important to remember that our heavenly Father has forgiven us. Therefore, we should not hesitate to forgive those who have wronged us and focus on a better tomorrow. Love is the most potent force, and God embodies this love. Forgiveness is an essential aspect of love and should be regarded as such. Even though it can be challenging to converse with someone who has wronged us, we must remember that forgiveness is a divine act. By forgiving those who have harmed us, we allow God's love to work through us and heal our hearts.

Sometimes, searching for a solution to a problem can be really stressful and emotionally challenging. However, this distress can sometimes lead us to find a solution. On the other hand, sometimes we might be trying to solve someone else's problem without realizing that we are the solution ourselves; we may be the answer to their prayer. Waiting for an answer for a long time can be painful. It's essential to be mindful of how we perceive the answer when it finally comes.

Sometimes, we kill the answer God sends to us. Don't kill your answer because you may not get another one. They killed Jesus, and after He was resurrected, He did not speak to the religious leaders again nor visit their temple. The Pharisees thought they knew God better than most and died only to find out they killed the answer. God had sent them The Answer when they thought He did not answer their prayers.

By holding onto faith and trust in God, we can find the strength to persevere. Jesus is our most outstanding example of how people may mistreat, misunderstand, and not appreciate us. However, God has sent us as someone's answer, just like Jesus, even if they don't know it or receive us.

We shouldn't take rejection personally. Jesus said, "When they reject you, they are rejecting Me and the Father who sent Me." Therefore, we should not be discouraged but rather shake the dust off our feet; that dust will be a testimony against them on the day of judgment. Our priority should be to obey God no matter how difficult it might seem.

Jesus taught us a powerful lesson on loving those who hate us. It's a difficult challenge that we must strive to achieve. Instead of destroying or judging others, we should leave that up to God. We may never know how our love and prayers could impact someone's life.

Our actions could be the only lesson of love they will ever see. Our daily challenge is to wake up with the expectation of being used by God to be someone's answer. By knowing and understanding Jesus, we can be The Answer for those who need it most.

"God so loved the world that He gave His only Son that whoever believes in Him will not perish but have eternal life."

When God gave us Jesus, He gave us The Answer!

Remember that trouble is a temporary state of being, no matter what you're going through or have suffered. It was not designed to last in this world, no matter the problem.

Have you ever wondered if the answer to a question or problem you've been pondering is already out there? The truth is, if we can think of a question, God already has the answer. With God, the answer always comes before the question. He knows the end from the beginning and is the Alpha and Omega, the Beginning and the End, the First and the Last. It's no coincidence that the scripture says, "The Lamb was slain before the foundations of the world."

This means that before humanity ever sinned, the solution to the problem was already in place. In other words, God had already provided the answer because He is the Answer.

Everything we need is in Him. He is the thirst and the water that quenches the thirst. He is the air we breathe and the lungs that desperately need it. He is the hunger and the food that satisfies. He is everything we need and more… *He Is God!*

Today, we are encountering several challenges and problems. I understand that people are looking for solutions and answers.

When we pray, we should strive to have faith in God and trust Him, knowing that whatever the issue, ultimately, **Jesus is The Answer!**

Prayer of Salvation

Scripture says, "Whoever calls upon the name of the Lord will be saved." If you would like to know Christ, you can receive the free gift of salvation through Jesus Christ by praying for salvation.

Please say this prayer out loud: "Oh merciful Lord Jesus, I humble myself before you and sincerely apologize for my transgressions. I acknowledge that I have strayed from your ways and ask for your forgiveness.

Please purify me of my sins and make me clean. I firmly believe that you are the Son of God, who sacrificed your life on the cross out of love for humanity to redeem us all. On the third day, you rose again, triumphant over death and sin, and bestowed the gift of eternal life upon us.

With all my heart, I profess that you are my Savior and Lord, and I pledge to follow you throughout my life.

Prayer for the New Beginner

Dear Heavenly Father,

As a new believer, I humbly come before you, seeking your guidance and grace on this faith journey. I am grateful for your Word that brings hope, strength, and assurance of your love for me. As I delve into the Scriptures, I pray that they become a lamp to my feet and a light to my path.

Please help me grow in my relationship with you and trust your plans for my life. May I find comfort in your presence, and may my life testify to your love for those around me.

I fervently pray in the name of our Lord and Savior, **_Jesus Christ_**. Amen.

Note: If you have recently embarked on this new chapter of faith, we rejoice with you and congratulate you on this significant step. We eagerly await hearing from you about your decision, praying with you, and providing you with the necessary materials and guidance as you begin your journey.

Prayer 1

Dear Father, we are grateful that you sent us the answer in the form of your Son, Jesus.

Dear Lord, we humbly ask for your divine wisdom and discernment to recognize the things that are meant to come from you. Please help us see your answers to our prayers, no

matter what form they take. We acknowledge our past mistakes of rejecting and mistreating your blessings and seek your forgiveness. May we never again miss an opportunity to receive your grace and mercy. Thank you for your unwavering love and guidance.
Amen.

Please grant us another chance to receive the answer that you've sent us. Help us to see what You see and guide us towards a path of righteousness in *Jesus's* name.

Prayer 2

As a devout Christian, I believe that the power of Jesus Christ is my ultimate salvation. Trusting in God is more than just a statement of faith; it's a testament to my unwavering commitment to following Jesus as my Lord and Savior.

Through prayer, I express my gratitude, confess my sins, and seek forgiveness and guidance. It's an intimate worship act that reflects my deep relationship with God and my unwavering desire to live according to his teachings. I pray that my faith in Jesus never wavers and that I may always walk in his light.

Contact us: Kingdomrights2.org

Info@kingdomrights2.org.

"My Father's House Shall Be Called A House Of Prayer."

7 MINUTES WITH GOD PRAYER

CHALLENGE

A place where we are laying down our phones and devices...yes, you heard me correctly, our smart phones and devices for just Seven (7) DEDICATED minutes with God.

Calling on all Prayer Warriors!
We have traded praying for great production.
We are in troubling times. The world and the church are falling apart; we must admit that we owe God an apology and must repent.
Wherever you are in this world, as believers let's agree to pray everyday

@ 7:00 a.m.

Whatever your time zone

INFO@KINGDOMRIGHTS2.ORG

LET'S PRAY!

Books. By Joseph Brice
Now Available:

- **Born Again Now What?**

- **Born Again Now What? Jesus Is The Resurrection**

- **Can A Woman Preach?**

- **God The Woman And Their Enemy**

- **Dios, La Mujer Y Su Enemigo**

- **Resurrection**

- **Why I Satan Hate The Woman**

These books are available in paperback, Hardcover, e-book and Audiobook.

- Available on Amazon, Barnes and Noble, Apple Books, Google Books, and Walmart Books.

- Also available on our Kingdom Store @kingdomrights2.org

✳ ✳ ✳

It is available now on Apple Podcast, Audible, Amazon Music, Spotify, Pandora, iHeart Radio, SiriusXM, and Google Podcast.

<u>Kingdom Podcast: See the Link Below</u>

When It's All Said And Done

<u>https://KingdomRights.sermon.net/main/main/22177375</u>

<u>Seven Minutes with God Podcast: See the Link Below</u>

Can A Woman Preach?

https://KingdomRights.sermon.net/22180281

ALL options are available on your Apple and Android App Store and Our own Kingdom Rights app.   Look for our Logo.

Kingdom Rights

Website: Kingdomrights2.org

Note from the Author

The enemy will constantly throw things at you to see what will hit. He doesn't know what will work or what won't; he's not God! His job is to destroy you by any means necessary.

The devil will pay you to allow him to destroy you. Every gift the enemy gives you, you will not be able to keep. Sometimes we can become so desperate for a blessing that we don't confirm the source and can end up with a curse.

The enemy is watching how we handle God's promises. The Holy Spirit is our helper if we want to be obedient, loyal, and dedicated to our Lord. Are you willing to risk your soul for temporary things in life?
Stay faithful to Jesus.